GW00505167

THE
FESTIVE FOOD
OF
FRANCE

Marie-Pierre Moine

ILLUSTRATED BY SALLY MALTBY

SERIES EDITOR: HENRIETTA GREEN

KYLE CATHIE LIMITED

Dedication
For Michèle Richet, with thanks and affection.

First published 1991 by
Kyle Cathie Limited
3 Vincent Square London SW1P 2LX

Copyright © 1991 by Marie-Pierre Moine
Illustrations copyright © 1991 by Sally Maltby

ISBN 1 85626 019 4

A CIP catalogue record for this book is available
from the British Library

Designed and typeset by Geoff Hayes
on his posh new AppleMac

Printed and bound in Belgium by
Proost International Book Production

Contents

La Fête des Rois

TWELFTH NIGHT

On January 6th children all over France go to school in happy anticipation of the final treat of the Christmas celebrations – *la Galette des Rois*. If they are lucky, children will eat it twice, at lunchtime in the school canteen and again at home in the evening.

What makes the almond puff pastry cake particularly exciting is that it conceals a small bean-like china token, a *fève*, which one lucky person will find in his wedge of *galette* (making a great show of nearly breaking a tooth or choking), and which makes him or her king or queen for the evening, complete with golden cardboard crown. Most people nowadays buy their *galette* from the local *pâtisserie,* but it always comes complete with token and crown.

Twelfth Night commemorates the visit of the three kings to the crib and marks the end of the Christmas festivities, but the idea of the lucky king of the feast goes back to wild rites and pre-Christian times, when the 'feast' the 'king' presided over tended to be a drunken and often bloody orgy – a far cry from the quiet family celebration it has become in France.

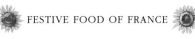

Galette des Rois

(TWELFTH NIGHT CAKE)

serves 6
300g/10½oz puff pastry
egg yolk and 1tablespoon/1½tablespoons milk
for glazing

Filling
170g/6oz/1½cups ground almonds
grated zest of 1 small orange
20ml/1tablespoon/1½tablespoons kirsch
100g/3½oz/½cup caster sugar
100g/3½oz/½cup unsalted butter, softened
small token (or ceramic bean)

1 Divide the puff pastry into two pieces and roll
out each piece into a circle, about 20–25cm/8–10in
in diameter. Line a baking sheet with greaseproof
paper and place one circle of pastry in the centre.
2 To prepare the filling, combine the ground
almonds, orange zest, kirsch, caster sugar and
butter until smooth.
3 Spread the filling evenly over the circle of
pastry, leaving a 2.5cm/1in border. Tuck the token
into the filling, somewhere halfway between the
centre and the edge.
4 Using a pastry brush, moisten the border of the
circle with a little glazing mixture. Carefully
position the second circle of puff pastry over the
first, pressing gently around the edge to seal it.
Prick the pastry in several places with a fork. Using
a sharp knife, cut a criss-cross pattern all over.
Brush the whole surface lightly with the rest of the
glazing mixture.
5 Bake for 20–30 minutes in a preheated 200°C/
400°F/gas6 oven until golden and puffed, taking
care not to open the oven door during the first 15
minutes. Serve warm.

La Fête des Omelettes

OMELETTE FEAST

Every year on February 10th after a long absence of nearly one hundred days the sun makes a welcome return to the tiny mountain village of Les Andrieux in the Hautes-Alpes of northern Provence. The inhabitants traditionally celebrate this long-awaited reappearance by making omelettes.

Omelette traditionnelle
(TRADITIONAL FRENCH OMELETTE)

serves 2
4 large eggs
20ml/1tablespoon/1½tablespoons water
30g/1oz butter
salt and freshly ground black pepper

1 Lightly beat the eggs with the water. Season to taste with salt and freshly ground black pepper.
2 Heat a small, heavy-based frying-pan. Add most of the butter to the hot pan, reserving a knob to finish the omelette. When the butter is very hot but not burning, pour in the egg mixture. Leave to settle for a moment, then start slowly stirring up the mixture towards the centre. As soon as the eggs begin to look just set but still moist, fold one quarter of the omelette towards the centre, then fold over the opposite side. Cook for a moment longer, then invert the omelette on a warmed serving plate. Trail the remaining butter over it and serve immediately.

Fillings for two 4-egg omelettes

Provençal vegetable

30ml/1½ tablespoons/2tablespoons olive oil

1 small red pepper, cored, deseeded and thinly
sliced

1 small bulb fennel, halved, trimmed and sliced
into thin segments

2 spring onions, finely chopped

½ garlic clove, finely chopped

sprig of fresh thyme or pinch of dried

salt and freshly ground black pepper

1 Heat the oil in a pan over a medium-high heat,
then add the prepared vegetables and the thyme.
Cook for about 10–15 minutes, stirring frequently
until the vegetables are soft and golden brown.
Season to taste.

2 Cook the omelettes and just before folding
spoon half the vegetables on the centre of each.

Jam

100ml/4fl oz/½cup apricot or raspberry jam, or
redcurrant jelly

10ml/2teaspoons brandy, *eau de vie* or liqueur

10ml/2teaspoons caster sugar for the omelettes

icing sugar for dredging

1 Combine the jam or jelly with the brandy or
liqueur.

2 Prepare the omelette as described opposite, but
adding the caster sugar and using only the tiniest
pinch of salt. Cook and fill as described, and dredge
with icing sugar just before serving.

Le Carnaval

CARNIVAL

The annual Carnival, preceding the forty lean days of Lent has always been celebrated with feasting and merry-making, and colourful parades and processions of floats and, in the north, gigantic mannequins.

In Paris the doomed star of Carnival was traditionally a huge ox, *le Bœuf Gras*. This carefully selected specimen could weigh over 1800 kilos/ 4000 pounds and its meat went to the master-butchers. Apprentices also had 'their' share of the beast. This they used to tie to a piece of string labelled with their name and cook in a vast communal pot. The young butchers' Carnival dish, *Bœuf Ficelle*, has remained one of the classics of French cooking.

Bœuf Ficelle

(BEEF POACHED IN STOCK)

serves 4

700g/1⅔lb piece of lean fillet or rumpsteak
1.1 litres/2pints/5cups light veal or beef stock
450g/1lb carrots, peeled and chopped
450g/1lb baby turnips, peeled and chopped
225g/8oz brown cap mushrooms, wiped and sliced
20ml/1tablespoon/1½tablespoons brandy
30g/1oz butter
40ml/2tablespoons/3tablespoons finely chopped
  flat-leaf parsley
coarse sea salt
black pepper
Dijon mustard

1 Bring the stock to the boil in a large saucepan. Add the carrots and turnips, reduce the heat and simmer for 10–12 minutes, then add the mushrooms and sprinkle with the brandy and continue simmering for 2–3 minutes.

2 Meanwhile, tie the beef securely with a piece of string long enough for you to hang it from the handle or handles of the pan during cooking.

3 Remove the vegetables from the pan with a slotted spoon and keep warm.

4 Bring the stock to the boil and carefully plunge the beef into the boiling liquid. Tie the string to the handles – the meat should not touch the bottom of the pan. Return to the boil, then simmer for about 20–25 minutes, depending on how well done you like your beef. If the piece of beef is long rather than chunky, it will cook faster, about 15–20 minutes.

5 Remove the beef from the stock and place on a warmed dish. Return the vegetables to the stock to reheat briefly. Discard the string and cut the beef into 4 slices. Dot with butter and sprinkle with parsley. Arrange the vegetables around the meat and moisten them with a little stock. Serve with coarse sea salt, black pepper and mustard. Save the rest of the stock for another recipe.

Mardi Gras

SHROVE TUESDAY

'If you want your wheat to stay free of black rot, you must eat pancakes on Shrove Tuesday.' Cooking and eating pancakes or fritters on the last day of Carnival was believed to bring you luck and to this day the family frying-pan is put to good use all over France on the evening of Mardi Gras.

Fritters come in many guises: flower blossoms in Provence where spring comes early, apples in Normandy, curd cheese in the centre are just three.

Mardi Gras pancakes are wafer-thin and sweet. They are served with butter, sugar and a dash of lemon, or more traditionally with soft brown sugar (*cassonade*), and thick cream.

Pâte à Crêpes Bretonne
(BRITTANY PANCAKES)

makes about 18

250g/8½oz/2cups flour
pinch of salt
1 large egg, lightly beaten
100g/3½oz/½cup
  caster sugar

milk
30g/1oz butter, melted
20ml/1tablespoon/
  1½tablespoons rum

1 Sift the flour and salt into a bowl. Work in the egg and sugar, then stir in enough milk to make a light, creamy batter. Stir in the melted butter and rum, and leave to rest for at least 20 minutes.
2 Just before cooking, stir a little extra milk or water into the batter if it looks too thick. Lightly grease a 12.5–15cm/5–6in pan, place it over a medium heat until hot, then spoon in 2–3 tablespoons batter. Swirl and cook for just over 1 minute on each side.

Beignets aux Pommes et au Cidre

(APPLE AND CIDER FRITTERS)

serves 6

250g/8½oz/2cups
  self-raising flour
pinch of salt
275g/9½oz/1⅙cups
  caster sugar, plus
  extra for sprinkling
finely grated zest of 1
  small lemon
100ml/4fl oz/½cup water
150ml/¼pint/⅔cup milk
20ml/1tablespoon/
  1½tablespoons sunflower
  or groundnut oil

250ml/⅓pint/1cup
  dry cider
550g/1¼lb eating apples
100ml/4fl oz/½cup
  Calvados or
  apple brandy
oil for deep-fat frying
cream, to serve

1 Sift the flour, salt, sugar (reserving 55g/2oz/
¼cup) and lemon zest into a large bowl, then
make a well in the centre. Combine the water,
milk, oil and cider and pour this liquid, a little at a
time, into the centre of the well. Stir in the dry
ingredients until you have a smooth batter. Cover
and leave to rest for 30 minutes.

2 Meanwhile, peel and core the apples, then cut
them into thick rings. Combine the rest of the sugar
with the Calvados or brandy and coat the apple
rings with the mixture.

3 Heat the oil in a deep frying-pan or deep-fat
fryer over a medium-high heat. When hot (about
180°C/350°F) dip the apple rings a few at a time in
the batter and fry them for about 3 minutes until
crisp and golden all over.

4 Drain well on absorbent paper. Sprinkle with a
little sugar and serve hot, with a jug of cream.

Foire au Boudin

BLACK PUDDING FAIR

The third weekend in March, the Black Pudding Fair, is the highlight of the year in the Normandy town of Mortagne-au-Perche. Hundreds of competitors from France and abroad enter their black puddings in the annual championship – by express post or in person – while people with hearty appetites prepare themselves to wolf down large quantities of the stuff in order to win the coveted title of champion *boudin* eater ...

There are as many types of *boudin* as there are butchers making it but it tends to be a spicy mixture of pig's blood and fat encased in gut and then poached. It is traditionally served pan-fried with fried apple slices and/or creamed potatoes.

Boudin Poêlé Sauce Moutarde
(PAN-FRIED BLACK PUDDING WITH MUSTARD SAUCE)
serves 2

200g/7oz French-style *boudin* or English black pudding
10ml/2teaspoons oil
30g/1oz butter
50ml/3tablespoons/¼cup dry white wine
20ml/1tablespoon/1½tablespoons thick cream
10ml/2teaspoons Dijon mustard
salt and freshly ground black pepper

1 If using *boudin*, cut it across into 2 pieces and prick several times with a fork. If using thicker black pudding, cut it into 2.5cm/1in slices, then remove the skin.
2 In a large frying-pan heat the oil and half the butter over a moderate heat. Reduce the heat and add the *boudin* or black pudding. Sauté gently. If using *boudin* cook for 12–15 minutes, turning the sausages over to cook them evenly. If using black pudding, cook for 5 minutes on each side. In either case keep the heat low to prevent the sausage disintegrating. Remove from the pan and keep warm.
3 Turn up the heat. Add the wine to the pan and stir with the pan juices until slightly reduced. Stir in the cream and mustard. Heat through, turn off the heat and whisk in the rest of the butter. Season lightly with salt and more generously with pepper. Spoon the sauce over the black pudding and serve immediately.

Vendredi Saint

GOOD FRIDAY

The most significant Friday of the year is Good Friday when the traditional Lenten dish *Brandade de Morue*, a pounded salt cod concoction, is served all over France.

As a predominantly Catholic country, France used to obey the Church's fasting rules very strictly. No meat was ever to be consumed on Fridays or during Lent and, if you wanted to eat butter on such 'lean' days, you had to give the church a special offering, which proved to be an excellent source of income.

Creamily fishy, *Brandade* is just the thing for eating on Good Friday: it keeps well and, served with potatoes and followed by a salad, is substantial enough to sustain people through the lengthy services and rigours of the day.

For the last two centuries salt cod, originally from Provence, has been easily available throughout France. It may be an acquired taste but devotees go to great lengths to indulge themselves.Monsieur Thiers, a nineteenth-century gourmand, statesman and briefly President of the Republic, was forbidden *Brandade* by his doctors. Undaunted and determined not to be deprived, he persuaded a fellow enthusiast to smuggle the dish into his office, hidden under official documents.

Brandade de Morue

(SALT COD PROVENÇALE)

serves 4

450g/1lb salt cod
bouquet garni
200ml/7fl oz olive oil
100ml/4fl oz/½cup milk
2–3 garlic cloves,
    finely chopped
75ml/5tablespoons/⅓cup
    thick cream

juice of 1 lemon
freshly ground black
    pepper, to taste
freshly grated nutmeg,
    to taste

1 Soak the salt cod overnight, preferably up to 12–14 hours, in plenty of cold water, changing the water several times to get rid of the saltiness.

2 Break the fish into chunks. Place in a large saucepan with the bouquet garni, cover with fresh cold water and bring to the boil. Reduce the heat and simmer very gently for 10–15 minutes without letting it boil as this would toughen the flesh.

3 Remove the flesh from the pan, drain it well and discard the skin and as many bones as possible. Then, in a large bowl, shred or mash the fish into small pieces.

4 Meanwhile, gently heat the olive oil and milk in separate pans. Pour half the warm olive oil over the fish and pound vigorously, using a large pestle or wooden spoon.

5 Work in the garlic, the remaining oil and the milk, a little at a time until you end up with a thick purée. This will probably take around 10 minutes.

6 Stir in the cream and lemon juice and season with the pepper and nutmeg. Return the mixture to a pan, add the butter and reheat gently. Serve with garlic croûtons.

La Foire aux Jambons

HAM FAIR

Everywhere in France the end of Lent has always meant indulging once more in dishes that are forbidden during lean days. What can be less lean than a rotund pig? The most celebrated ham fair, *La Foire aux Jambons*, used to take place in Paris around the time of Holy Week. It still takes place but has moved from its grand setting in front of Notre Dame to the more modest suburb of Chatou.

One of the most delectable of the ham dishes originated in Burgundy. *Jambon Persillé*, cubes of ham set in a white wine jelly, has become the *specialité de la maison* of many a *charcuterie* of the region. At Easter it is served in a round white china bowl, sometimes with hardboiled eggs set inside the hams, a seasonal touch. Festive cooking is not for people with small appetites, particularly in Burgundy, where *Jambon Persillé* tends to be eaten as a starter, with pickled gherkins and bread. It is substantial enough to make a satisfying and attractive main course, served with a salad.

Jambon Persillé
(JELLIED HAM WITH PARSLEY)

serves 8

1.5kg/3½lb piece of gammon or ham, rinsed
beef marrow bone or veal knuckle, chopped in half
2 calves' feet, split
1 Spanish onion studded with 4 cloves
2 each of shallots and carrots
bouquet garni
a few sprigs of chervil and tarragon

pinch each of dried marjoram and tarragon
8 black peppercorns
700ml/1¼pints/3cups dry white wine
200g/7oz finely chopped flat-leaf parsley
20ml/1tablespoon/1½tablespoons white wine
    vinegar
freshly ground black pepper

1 Rinse the gammon or ham. Put it in a large
saucepan, cover with water and bring to the boil
over a moderate heat. Simmer for 30 minutes.
2 Remove the meat from the pan. Discard the
cooking liquid and rinse out the pan. Divide the
meat into 4 pieces. Cut out and discard any rind or
excessively fatty bits.
3 Return the meat to the pan, with the beef
marrow or veal knuckle, the calves' feet, onion,
shallots, carrots, bouquet garni, herbs and peppercorns. Pour in the wine. Bring to the boil over a low
heat, cover and simmer very gently for 2 hours,
skimming off any fat from time to time.
4 Leave to cool, remove the meat with a slotted
spoon and put into a large bowl. Strain the
cooking liquid through a sieve and keep warm.
5 Using two forks, lightly flake the meat. Stir in 2
tablespoons of the parsley and the vinegar. Season
to taste with freshly ground black pepper.
6 In a wetted salad bowl or a 1.1litre/2pint/5cup
loaf tin, sprinkle a layer of chopped parsley, then
spread a layer of flaked meat over, and continue
alternating, ending up with a thick layer of parsley.
7 Trickle the cooking liquid into the dish, allowing
it to seep under the parsley. Cover, place a weight
on top and set overnight in the refrigerator.
8 Serve in the bowl or turned out. To turn out the
jellied ham, soak a tea towel in hot water, wring it
out and wrap it around the base of the bowl or tin
for a minute. Invert onto a plate. The jellied ham
will keep for several days in the refrigerator.

Pâques
EASTER

On Easter morning, when church bells are ringing out all over the country, French children are busy looking for Easter eggs hidden around the garden or house before the traditional family lunch. The symbol of new life, eggs have always been at the heart of Easter celebrations, and eggs laid on Good Friday were thought to have magic properties. In our commercial era Easter eggs tend to come in shop-bought chocolate form, but for centuries they were plainly hardboiled. Children and youths begged for eggs from door to door and played ritual games with them. They were rolled down long planks, rather like *boules*, and the winner's egg was the one that remained intact. The eggs were then chopped into salads or pies. In the south-east tinted hardboiled eggs are still embedded in ring-shaped sweet cakes which children wear as edible armlets.

For many French families an Easter feast would be incomplete without an expensive *gigot pascal*, a roast leg of lamb. Dried haricot beans simmered until tender are a traditional accompaniment in the west of the country. In the north-east where fewer sheep are raised, the great Easter symbol is a lamb-shaped cake rather than an actual roast...

Œufs en Chocolat
(CHOCOLATE EGGS)

makes 6

6 small or medium eggs (plus a few spares in case of accidents)

500g/1lb/2oz dark, milk or white chocolate (or a combination of the three), plus extra for decoration (optional)

candied angelica leaves for decoration (optional)

1 Holding an egg very carefully in one hand, delicately pierce a small hole at both ends with a needle. Gently blow out the contents of the egg (you may find it helpful to insert a short straw into one end and blow into the straw). Carefully enlarge one hole until it is about 5mm/¼in wide. Wash the egg under running cold water and leave to drain. Repeat the operation with the remaining eggs.

2 Once the shells are completely dry stick a small piece of foil over each of the small holes (using sticky tape rather than glue).

3 Break the chocolate into a small bowl (use as many bowls as you have types of chocolate). Place the bowl over a saucepan of simmering water and melt the chocolate, stirring occasionally.

4 Once the chocolate has completely melted, carefully spoon it into the egg shells through the larger holes, making sure that there are no air bubbles. If you prefer, slowly trickle the chocolate into the shells with the help of a small funnel. Refrigerate the eggs for a few hours until set.

5 Gently crack the shells and remove to reveal the chocolate eggs. If you like, decorate the eggs with trimmed angelica leaves by sticking them to the eggs with a little melted chocolate.

Gigot aux Flageolets

(LEG OF LAMB WITH HARICOT BEANS)

serves 6

1 part-boned leg of new-season lamb, trimmed
  French style, weighing about 1.8kg/4lb
900g/2lb dried flageolet or white haricot beans,
  soaked overnight
3 large Spanish onions, peeled
5 garlic cloves
bouquet garni
a few springs of thyme
2 bay leaves
85g/3oz/⅓cup butter
5 shallots
2 ripe tomatoes, skinned, deseeded and chopped
100ml/4fl oz/½cup dry white wine
salt and freshly ground black pepper

1 Bring to the boil a large saucepan of cold water
with the soaked beans. Drain well, return to the
pan, cover with boiling water and add 2 onions, 1
garlic clove, the bouquet garni, sprigs of thyme and
bay leaves. Bring back to the boil and simmer for
at least 1½ hours, seasoning with salt and pepper
after 1 hour. The beans should be just soft but not
collapsing. Test occasionally, because the exact
timing depends on the beans you use. Drain.
2 Meanwhile, bring the leg of lamb to room
temperature. Heat the oven and a roasting tin to
230°C/450°F/gas8. Cut the rest of the garlic cloves
into slivers. Using a small sharp knife, make small
cuts in the meat and push in the garlic slivers. Dot
with 30g/1oz butter and season liberally with salt
and pepper. Roast the lamb, allowing 12–16
minutes for each 450g/1lb, depending on how pink
you like your lamb to be.
3 Prepare a sauce. Finely chop the last onion and
the shallots. Melt the rest of the butter in a small
saucepan, and sweat the prepared onion and

shallots gently without letting them brown. Add the prepared tomatoes and cook slowly until soft, then add half the wine, season lightly and continue cooking for a few minutes.

4 Once the lamb is cooked, pour half its cooking juices into the sauce mixture. Spread the beans in a large gratin dish. Pour the sauce mixture over the beans and stir gently until they are well soaked. Put the lamb on top of the beans and place the dish in the oven. Turn off the heat after 5 minutes and leave to stand in the hot oven for a further 10 minutes.

5 While the dish is settling in the oven, pour the rest of the wine into the roasting tin, stir with the remaining cooking juices over a brisk heat, then strain into a sauceboat and serve with the lamb.

Salade aux Pissenlits
(DANDELION SALAD)

serves 6

250g/8½oz dandelion leaves, trimmed, rinsed and drained
100g/3½oz lettuce leaves, trimmed, rinsed and drained
20ml/1tablespoon/1½tablespoons white or red wine vinegar
75ml/5tablespoons/⅓cup light olive oil
garlic croûtons
1 hardboiled egg, chopped
6 black olives, stoned and chopped
salt and freshly ground black pepper

1 Combine the vinegar and oil and season with salt and pepper to taste.

2 Pour this dressing over the salad leaves and toss until well coated. Sprinkle in the croûtons, chopped hardboiled egg and olives. Toss again lightly, check seasoning and serve.

Saint Honoré

The namedays of saints feature prominently on the colourful calendar issued by the post office which has become a national institution to be seen hanging in most French kitchens. It is a reminder that every craft and profession traditionally has its own patron; May 16th is the Feast of Saint-Honoré, patron saint of bakers, traditionally portrayed holding the long-handled oven peel, or shovel, of his trade.

This elaborate choux paste and cream concoction is named after him.

Gâteau Saint Honoré
(ST HONORE'S CAKE)

serves 6–8
225g/8oz shortcrust
  pastry
1tablespoon
  1½tablespoons
  caster sugar
10ml/2teaspoons
  ground almonds

Choux paste
150ml/¼pint/⅔cup water
55g/2oz/¼cup butter, diced
pinch of salt
75g/2½oz/¾cup flour
2 large eggs, beaten
few drops of
  vanilla essence

Glaze
1 small egg and a little milk, beaten

Crème Chantilly
400ml/⅔pint/1¾cups
  double cream
icing sugar to taste
20ml/1 tablespoon/
  1½tablespoons
  iced water
10ml/2 teaspoons
  kirsch

Caramel Syrup
100g/3½oz/½cup
  caster sugar
50ml/3tablespoons/
  ¼cup water

1 Roll out the shortcrust pastry into a thin 20cm/ 8in circle. Sprinkle it with the sugar and ground almonds, pressing in lightly. Spread the circle on a greased baking sheet and chill for 20 minutes.

2 To make the choux paste, bring the water, diced butter and salt to the boil in a heavy-based saucepan. Remove the boiling liquid from the heat and quickly stir in the flour with a wooden spoon. Return to a medium-hot heat and stir briskly until the paste is shiny and comes off the sides of the pan. Beat in the eggs until the paste is glossy. Flavour with a few drops of vanilla essence.

3 Fit a piping bag with a plain 1cm/½in nozzle and pipe a ring of paste around the chilled pastry circle 5mm/¼in from the edge.

4 Use the rest of the choux paste to pipe small puffs onto a second greased baking sheet, keeping them well apart. Brush the choux paste circle and puffs lightly with glaze.

5 Bake the ring and the small puffs for 10 minutes in a preheated 220°C/425°F/gas7 oven, then open the oven door for a minute, turn down the heat to 190°C/375°F/gas5 and bake for a further 10–15 minutes until firm and dry. Leave to cool on a rack.

6 Make the Crème Chantilly. Whisk the cream. Sift in icing sugar to taste, then beat until stiff. Fold in the iced water and kirsch. Slit open the puffs and spoon in a little Crème Chantilly. Chill the choux and the rest of the cream until needed. Prepare the caramel syrup. In a small saucepan heat the sugar in the water until the sugar has dissolved, stirring constantly. Boil until the syrup thickens and turns a pale gold. Remove from the heat. Using tongs, quickly and carefully dip the choux puffs into the syrup, then arrange them on top of the choux paste ring. Spoon the rest of the Crème Chantilly into the centre of the cake and serve as soon as possible, or keep chilled until needed.

Foires aux Asperges

ASPARAGUS FAIRS

Wherever asparagus happens to be the pride of the local produce, the start of the new season is a happy occasion. Many villages hold an asparagus fair, where growers proudly display the best of their crop to a gallery of critical experts. For the French, asparagus is the most highly prized of vegetables. Everybody has strong views about the precious stalks – which variety tastes best, how to accommodate it and whether to serve it hot, warm or cold. In the Sologne area of the Loire where it was introduced by a retired policeman just over a century ago, asparagus even have their own fan club, La Confrérie des Mangeux d'Esparges, the brotherhood of asparagus-eaters. Twice a year members put on purple robes trimmed with white and solemnly meet to enjoy a good meal and talk about *asperges*.

Asperges au Naturel
(PLAIN-COOKED ASPARAGUS)

serves 4

550g/1¼lb asparagus   salt

1 Trim the asparagus of woody ends and tough fibrous skin if necessary. Rinse well. Tie the stalks in bundles and stand the bundles in glass jars. Fill with boiling salted water to just below the tips, cover with foil and place in a large, deep pan of simmering water. Cook until the asparagus feel just tender when pierced with a knife below the tips. This will take 10–35 minutes, depending on the asparagus.

2 Drain well on a clean thick tea towel and serve warm, with lemon butter or anchovy vinaigrette.

Beurre Citronné

(LEMON BUTTER)

40ml/2tablespoons/3tablespoons water
100g/3½oz/½cup butter
juice of ½ small lemon
salt and white pepper

Bring the water to the boil in a small saucepan.
Remove from the heat, swirl in the butter until
melted and season to taste with a little salt, pepper
and lemon juice.

Vinaigrette à l'Anchois

(ANCHOVY VINAIGRETTE)

100ml/4fl oz/½cup light olive oil
40ml/2tablespoons/3tablespoons red wine vinegar
1–2 anchovy fillets, drained of oil and mashed, or
    1teaspoon anchovy essence
freshly ground black pepper
a few sprigs each of flat-leaf parsley, chives,
    tarragon and/or chervil

Whisk together the olive oil, vinegar, mashed
anchovy fillets or anchovy essence. Season to taste
with pepper. Snip the fresh herbs and stir them
into the vinaigrette.

Le Temps des Cerises

THE CHERRY SEASON

Quand reviendra le temps des cerises... when it is cherry time again, according to the song, people's thoughts turn to romance and jollity. Villages everywhere make merry at cherry festivals and *Clafoutis* (from the French patois, *clafir*, to garnish) takes pride of place in the front windows of the *pâtisseries*. This cherry custard pudding is one of the most traditional of France's fruit desserts. The stones are normally left in the cherries, which does great things for the flavour of the pudding but may be hazardous for young children and people unfamiliar with this dish.

In some regions it is baked on top of a large buttered cabbage leaf – but it does taste just as good cooked in a more conventional container! When the cherry season is over, this favourite French dessert is worth making with plums (stoned and halved) or apples (cored and quartered).

Clafoutis
(CHERRY CUSTARD PUDDING)

serves 6

800g/1¾lb ripe red or black cherries, washed and
   stalks removed
100g/3½oz/½cup flour
pinch of salt
200g/7oz/1cup caster sugar
3 large eggs
700ml/1¼pints/3cups milk
20ml/1tablespoon/1½tablespoons kirsch
butter for greasing

1 Sift the flour with a pinch of salt into a large
bowl. Stir in the sugar, reserving 3 tablespoons.
Work in the eggs, one at a time, beating them in
well with a wooden spoon.
2 Trickle in the milk, very slowly to begin with,
stirring well to prevent lumps forming. Flavour
with the kirsch.
3 Butter a large gratin dish. Arrange the cherries in
the dish, cover with the batter and bake for 40–45
minutes in a preheated 200°C/400°F/gas6 oven,
until set and golden.

4 Sprinkle with the
reserved sugar and
leave to cool a little
before serving.

Foire au Fromage de Chèvre

GOAT'S CHEESE FAIR

Goat's cheese is one of the *specialités* of the Loire and every year in early June cheese-makers from the region and further afield converge on Sainte-Maure in Touraine, a town famous for its fine-flavoured farmhouse cheeses. Competitors enter their cheese in the *concours*, the very tough, nationally famous championship, in the hope of winning the coveted gold trophy.

Salade au Fromage de Chèvre
(GOAT'S CHEESE SALAD)

serves 4
40ml/2tablespoons/3tablespoons olive oil
125g/4½oz moist goat's cheese
50ml/3tablespoons/¼cup grapeseed or sunflower oil
20ml/1tablespoon/1½tablespoons red or white wine vinegar
250g/8½oz mixed salad leaves
several sprigs of flat-leaf parsley, finely chopped croûtons, to serve
salt and freshly ground black pepper

1 In a frying-pan gently heat half the olive oil. Remove the crust from the cheese and cut into 8–12 small pieces. Sauté the cheese over a low heat until warm and lightly golden all over.

2 Pour the rest of the olive oil, the sunflower oil and the vinegar into the salad bowl. Stir well to blend, then season to taste with salt and pepper. Add the washed and dried salad leaves and parsley, and toss well. Place the sautéed cheese on top and serve at once with croûtons.

Croûtes au Fromage de Chèvre
(CHEESE CROUSTADES)

serves 4

100g/3½oz moist goat's cheese
20ml/1tablespoon/1½tablespoons cream or
   fromage frais
10ml/2teaspoons dry white wine
a few sprigs of chervil, finely chopped
4 slices of granary or other good bread, crusts
   removed
knob of butter
freshly ground black pepper

1 Using a fork, mash together the cheese, cream and wine. Season generously with pepper and mix in the herbs.
2 Lightly toast the bread on one side. Butter the untoasted side and spread the cheese mixture on top. Grill for a few minutes until bubbly and golden, and serve piping hot.

Pur Chèvre

9,50F

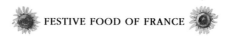

Foire à la Quiche Lorraine

BACON QUICHE FAIR

Perhaps less famous than neighbouring Alsace, the province of Lorraine in the north-east of the country has nevertheless given France many celebrated dishes and delicacies. Best known of all is the savoury bacon, cream and egg tart known as *Quiche Lorraine*. The dish has its own colourful fair every second year during the third weekend of June, in the small town of Dombasle-sur-Meurthe, not far from Nancy.

Quiche Lorraine
(BACON QUICHE)

serves 6

250g/8½oz shortcrust pastry
250g/8½oz thick cut rindless smoked streaky bacon
10ml/2teaspoons oil
30g/1oz butter, plus extra for greasing
3 large eggs
150ml/¼pint/⅔cup thick cream
ground nutmeg
salt and freshly ground black pepper

1 Roll out the pastry thinly and line a buttered
25cm/10in loose-bottomed tart tin, pressing it in
lightly with your hands. Prick all over with a fork.
Cover the pastry base with a piece of foil and dried
beans, then bake in a preheated 190°C/375°F/gas5
oven for 15 minutes. Remove the foil and beans.
2 Meanwhile, blanch the bacon in boiling water.
Drain well and pat dry with absorbent paper. Cut
into small pieces.
3 Heat the oil in a frying-pan and sauté the bacon
pieces until they are evenly crisp and golden. Drain
well on absorbent paper.
4 Spread the bacon pieces over the pastry base.
Arrange dots of butter in between the bacon
pieces.
5 Beat together the eggs and cream. Season very
lightly with salt (the bacon is salty) and nutmeg,
and liberally with pepper. Pour the mixture into
the pastry case and bake for about 20 minutes,
until set and golden brown. (Pierce with a fork
during baking if the filling swells unevenly.) Serve
warm rather than piping hot.

La Saint-Jean

MIDSUMMER

Gone are the days when bonfires lit up the skies of the French countryside on the night of Midsummer. Alas people no longer believe that jumping over a fire will bring good luck or prevent warts... Yet around June 23rd many country fairs and traditional local festivities still celebrate the *Saint Jean* – the midsummer festival and the name day of St John the Baptist. The town of Uzès holds a garlic festival, at which, as at the many other garlic fairs that take place all over France throughout the summer, stacks and bundles of bulbs pile up on tables and barrows and cafés do a roaring trade. The air takes on a lightly pungent aroma – one that Alexandre Dumas thought was 'good for you to breathe'. In some villages the highlight of the occasion is the crowning of the Garlic Queen and the communal partaking of bowls of steaming garlic soup... Of the following dishes the one with the most intense garlic flavour is the *Aïoli*. For a gentler effect, blanch the cloves first as explained in the chicken recipe.

Soupe à l'Ail

(VEGETABLE AND GARLIC SOUP)

serves 6

20ml/1tablespoon/1½tablespoons olive oil

225g/8oz rindless smoked streaky bacon, chopped

450g/1lb each of carrots and potatoes, peeled and finely chopped

2 Spanish onions, finely chopped

250g/8½oz swedes or turnips, peeled and finely chopped

2 courgettes, chopped

4–6 garlic cloves, peeled and chopped
1.3litres/2¼pints/6cups warm chicken or vegetable
    stock, or a mixture of stock and water
few sprigs of thyme and marjoram
1–2 bay leaves
2 large tomatoes, coarsely chopped
1 small can flageolets or cannellini beans, drained
salt and freshly ground black pepper

To serve
garlic croûtons
freshly grated Parmesan,
    Gruyère or strong Cheddar

1 In a large, heavy-based saucepan, heat the oil and
sauté the bacon pieces until golden. Add the
prepared vegetables and garlic, reserving the
tomatoes and beans, and sauté for a few minutes,
stirring frequently, until they colour.
2 Pour in the stock, season lightly with salt and
pepper and add the herbs and bay leaves. Cover
and cook very gently for 1 hour.
3 Add the tomatoes and beans and cook for a
further 15 minutes.
4 Check the seasoning. Remove the sprigs of
herbs and bay leaves. Serve piping hot with garlic
croûtons and freshly grated cheese.

Aïoli

makes 500ml/16fl oz/2cups
1tablespoon/1½tablespoons stale breadcrumbs,
    moistened with milk and squeezed
4–6 garlic cloves, peeled and mashed
2 egg yolks at room temperature
400ml/⅔pint/1¾cups olive oil at room temperature
1tablespoon/1½tablespoons boiling water
a few drops of lemon juice
salt and freshly ground black pepper

To serve
a selection of cold cooked vegetables and
   hard-boiled eggs
cold poached salt cod
leftover lamb or roast chicken

1 In a large bowl, combine the bread, mashed garlic
and egg yolks and season lightly with salt and
pepper.
2 Beat in the olive oil, a few drops at a time to
begin with, then in a thin trickle as for mayonnaise.
3 Once all the oil has been incorporated in the
aïoli, beat in the boiling water. Check the
seasoning and beat in a few drops of lemon juice
to taste. Cover with cling film and chill until ready
to use. Serve with cold cooked vegetables and
hardboiled eggs, fish, lamb or chicken.

Poulet Rôti à l'Ail
(ROAST CHICKEN WITH GARLIC)

This rich, golden chicken is good with French beans
and sautéed potatoes.

serves 4–6
1 oven-ready free-range or corn-fed chicken,
   weighing approximately 2.3kg/4–5lbs
450g/1lb young garlic cloves
a few sprigs each of thyme, rosemary, marjoram
   and/or oregano
40ml/2tablespoons/3tablespoons olive oil
30g/1oz butter
50ml/3tablespoons/¼cup dry white wine
50ml/3tablespoons/¼cup chicken stock
salt and freshly ground black pepper

1 Bring the chicken to room temperature.

2 Blanch the unpeeled garlic cloves in boiling water for 5–7minutes. Drain and plunge into cold water. Drain again. Squeeze each clove between your thumb and forefinger to peel off the skin.

3 Season the chicken inside and out with salt and pepper. Insert some of the herbs between the skin and the flesh and push the rest into the cavity. Put the chicken into a roasting dish. Tuck the prepared garlic under the bird and sprinkle with the olive oil. Dot with half the butter.

4 Roast the chicken for 40 minutes in a preheated 220°C/425°F/gas7 oven, basting and turning occasionally. Turn down the heat to 180°C/350°F/gas4 and continue roasting for a further 40 minutes or until cooked. Turn off the heat. Pour the cooking juices (but not the garlic) into a small pan and return the chicken and garlic to the oven.

5 Stir the wine and stock into the cooking juices and bring to a boil. Simmer the sauce for a few minutes until slightly reduced, then remove from the heat. Check the seasoning and stir in the rest of the butter.

6 Serve the chicken with the roasted garlic, and the sauce on the side.

Les Olivades

OLIVE FESTIVAL

The town of Nyons in the Drôme shares with Nice the honour of producing the best olives in France – small, firm and flavour packed. Every year in mid-July the olive festival, Les Olivades (from a provençal word meaning olive picking), solemnly opens with the resplendent Knights of the Olive Tree parading through the town.

The olive plays a vital part in the cooking of Provence. *Pan Bagna* – literally bathed bread – is the region's sunny version of the sandwich, and *Olives Cassées*, flavoured split olives, are traditionally nibbled with a glass of *pastis* or other apéritif.

Pan Bagna

(PROVENÇAL SANDWICH)

serves 2

2 large round bread rolls
1 garlic clove, peeled and halved
olive oil
2 ripe tomatoes (skinned and deseeded, if liked), thickly sliced
a few rings of mild white onion, or the white parts of 2 spring onions
8 black olives, stoned and coarsely chopped
2–4 basil leaves, finely chopped
2 sprigs of flat-leaf parsley, finely chopped
salt and freshly ground black pepper

1 Split the bread rolls and rub the insides with the
cut sides of the garlic clove. Sprinkle generously
with olive oil until the bread is well coated.
2 Fill with slices of tomato, rings of onion and olive
pieces. Sprinkle with chopped basil and parsley.
Season lightly with salt and pepper.
3 Wrap closely in a tea towel or kitchen paper and
leave at room temperature for at least 30 minutes
before eating.

Olives Cassées

(FLAVOURED SPLIT OLIVES)

300g/10½oz green olives
125g/4½oz sea salt
3 bay leaves
20ml/1tablespoon/1½tablespoons coarsely crushed
  coriander seeds
10ml/2teaspoons coarsely crushed fennel seeds
1litre/1¾pints/4½cups water
a couple of dried fennel stalks
olive oil, to serve

1 Bruise the olives with a small hammer or pestle
without crushing them. Plunge them in plenty of
cold water and leave to soak for 5 days, changing
the water every day.
2 In a clean jar, combine the drained olives, salt,
bay leaves, coriander and fennel seeds. Cover with
the water and shake well. Top with the fennel
stalks. Cover and leave to infuse for a week before
using.
3 Drain well and sprinkle lightly with olive oil
before serving.

Fête des Pommiers

APPLE TREE FESTIVAL

Brittany has always been apple country. In the old days the twenty or so local varieties of apple were seldom eaten raw. For young people one of the highlights of the year was the *queïserie*, the big apple cook–up, when apples were slowly simmered with sweet cider in large cauldrons while dancing went on through the night and romance blossomed.

Bretons and visitors can still get a taste of traditional cider, cakes and music during the third week of July in Finistère, at the Fouesnant apple tree festival. The farmhouse cider competition on the Saturday is followed on Sunday by a colourful fair, with folkloric floats, traditional costumes and a fireworks display at night.

42

Gâteau Breton aux Pommes
(BRITTANY APPLE CAKE)

serves 8
Filling
450g/1lb Cox's orange pippin or Egremont russet
  apples, peeled, cored and chopped
30g/1oz butter
1tablespoon/1½tablespoons sultanas
20ml/1tablespoon/1½tablespoons Calvados or
  apple brandy

Cake
200g/7oz/1cup caster sugar
6 medium or 4 large egg yolks
200g/7oz/1cup butter, softened, plus extra for
  greasing
20ml/1tablespoon/1½tablespoons Calvados
450g/1lb/4cups self-raising flour
20ml/1tablespoon/1½tablespoons milk, for glazing

1 To prepare the filling, melt the butter in a
saucepan, then stir in the prepared apples, sultanas
and Calvados. Cook over a low heat, stirring
occasionally, until the apples are soft.
2 Meanwhile, pour the sugar into a large bowl, and
whisk in the egg yolks, one at a time, until the
mixture is smooth and forms ribbons. Reserve a
little yolk for glazing. Work in the butter and the
Calvados, then sift in the flour, a little at a time.
3 Butter a deep, round loose-bottomed 20cm/8in
cake tin. Pour in half the cake mixture, spreading it
evenly with a spatula. Cover with the softened
apples. Top with the rest of the cake mixture and
smooth with a spatula. Combine the reserved yolk
with the milk and brush lightly over the cake.
4 Bake for about 45 minutes in a preheated 190°C/
375°F/gas5 oven, until cooked through and golden.
Remove from the tin and serve cold.

Pèlerinage de Notre-Dame du Rosaire

PILGRIMAGE OF OUR LADY OF THE ROSARY

Every year on September 8th the people of Bonifacio in Southern Corsica walk in pilgrimage to the Ermitage de la Trinité, a small convent a few kilometres from the town. After honouring Our Lady of the Rosary they traditionally eat a dish of stuffed aubergines, *Aubergines à la Bonifacienne.*

Aubergines Farcies à la Bonifacienne
(CORSICAN STUFFED AUBERGINES)

serves 4–6

3 even-sized plump unblemished large aubergines
60g/2oz/⅔cup 2-day-old breadcrumbs, soaked in a little milk and squeezed dry
2–3 garlic cloves, mashed
several leaves of fresh basil, finely chopped
2 medium eggs
15g/½oz butter, softened
45g/1½oz/¾cup freshly grated Parmesan
olive oil for frying
salt and freshly ground black pepper

Tomato Sauce
20ml/1tablespoon/1½tablespoons olive oil
½ mild Spanish onion, finely chopped
450g/1lb ripe tomatoes, blanched, peeled, deseeded and chopped
a pinch each of dried thyme and oregano
2 anchovy fillets, drained and mashed
salt and freshly ground black pepper

1 Cut the aubergines in half lengthways. Bring to the boil a large saucepan of lightly salted water. Add the aubergines and simmer them for 10 minutes, until part-cooked. Drain and leave to cool in a colander.

2 Meanwhile, prepare the tomato sauce. Heat the olive oil, add the onion and sauté over a low heat for a few minutes until softened, stirring frequently. Add the tomatoes, dried herbs and anchovy fillets. Cook gently until mushy, stirring occasionally. Liquidize and check the seasoning.

3 Squeeze the aubergines to extract as much water as possible. Scoop out the flesh, taking care not to pierce the skin. Squeeze the flesh again – it can never be too dry – then chop it finely. Reserve the shells, upside-down on a clean tea towel or absorbent paper.

4 In a bowl combine the prepared aubergine flesh, breadcrumbs, garlic and basil. Season generously with pepper, then work in the eggs, one at a time, and the butter. Stir in the grated Parmesan.

5 Spoon the filling into the aubergine shells.

6 In a large frying-pan heat a little olive oil. Starting with the filled side down, sauté the aubergines until cooked through and crispy brown. Add a little oil as necessary and keep the heat moderate. Serve hot, warm or cold with the tomato sauce.

Les Vendanges

During late September and early October, when the days are still hot but a misty chill hangs over the mornings and evenings, sleepy villages all over France suddenly come to life, and buzz with activity and noise... This is wine harvest time, when the owners of the vineyards marshall their troops – family, friends, hired help from far and near – and deploy them among the rows of vines to pick the precious grapes. Timing is crucial, so the pace is fast and the work arduous, but the atmosphere is happy and convivial – especially if the crop is a good one.

Every meal is a feast with the boss's wife dispensing huge comforting stews to the hungry wine-harvesters. Stews vary with the regions, but one that is traditionally served, and not just in the area it is named after, is *Bœuf Bourguignon*, the great beef and red wine casserole of Burgundy. It is dished out without ceremony, straight from the pot, when the grape-pickers, *les vendangeurs*, come in from toiling in the vineyards. In Burgundy the beef simmers in the rich red local wine, preferably Hautes–Côtes de Beaune, but outside the province this may be replaced by a bottle of the most appropriate red the region has to offer.

The portions are generous, but wine harvest meals are simple. Only one plate is used for each guest, mopped clean of juices after each course with a piece of bread. A typical meal will start with a hot vegetable soup or tomato salad. *Bœuf Bourguignon* is invariably accompanied by mountains of boiled potatoes, and followed by a green salad, then local cheeses. The dessert tends to be fruit or an open fruit tart.

Bœuf Bourguignon
(BEEF AND RED WINE CASSEROLE)

serves 4–6

1kg/2¼lb lean stewing steak
3 thick rindless slices fatty smoked bacon
2 large Spanish onions
2tablespoons/3tablespoons flour
700ml/1¼pints/3cups full-bodied red wine
bouquet garni
2 sage leaves
2 garlic cloves
18 button onions
30g/1oz butter
boiled or steamed potatoes, to serve
salt and freshly ground black pepper

1 Cut the beef into 5cm/2in cubes and chop up
the bacon. Heat a heavy-based casserole and brown
the bacon over a moderate heat.
2 Chop the Spanish onions, add them to the bacon
and stir over the heat until golden. Remove the
sautéed mixture with a slotted spoon and reserve.
3 Turn up the heat a little, add the beef to the pan
and sauté the pieces until evenly browned.
Sprinkle the meat with the flour and allow to
colour for a minute or two.
4 Pour in the wine. Add the bouquet garni, sage
leaves and whole cloves of garlic. Season to taste
with salt and pepper. Return the bacon and onion
mixture to the casserole. Cover tightly and simmer
very gently for 1¾hours, stirring once or twice.
5 Meanwhile, peel the button onions, then heat the
butter in a small frying-pan and the sauté the onions
until golden.
6 Add the onions to the casserole, stir, cover again
and continue cooking for another ¾ hour.
7 Serve the stew piping hot from the casserole
with boiled or steamed potatoes.

La Toussaint

ALL SAINTS' DAY

November 1st, All Saints, is a public holiday in France. It is the eve of *Le Jour des Morts*, All Souls, and the time when the dead are remembered. Village church bells used to toll all night while people held a wake and said prayers. They sustained themselves seasonally with freshly picked chestnuts and the first of the harvest's young wines. Customs and superstitions varied from region to region, but there was a widely held belief that for each chestnut you roasted in the fire and ate, a soul was saved from purgatory.

Chestnuts have always been an important foodstuff in France, particularly in the southern half of the country, where their trees were once known as 'bread trees'. Innumerable chestnut fairs still take place in the autumn in the run-up to the *Toussaint*. The soup recipe below comes from the Limousin where it was typical rural fare.

Soupe aux Châtaignes
(CHESTNUT SOUP)

serves 6
400g/14oz large chestnuts
5ml/1teaspoon oil
1.5litres/2½pints/6¼cups water
2 Spanish onions, coarsely chopped
2 leeks, trimmed, washed and sliced
1 large waxy potato, peeled and chopped
125ml/4½fl oz/⅔cup single cream
30g/1oz butter
salt and freshly ground black pepper

1 Nick the shells of the chestnuts with a sharp knife. Put them in a large saucepan with a pinch of salt and the oil. Cover with water and bring to the boil, then simmer for 10 minutes. Drain the chestnuts and remove the shells and inner skin as soon as they are cool enough to handle.

2 Rinse the pan. Pour in the water and add the prepared chestnuts and vegetables. Season with a little salt and pepper, then slowly bring to the boil and simmer gently for 40 minutes, or until the chestnuts and vegetables are cooked.

3 Pass the chestnuts and vegetables through a mouli, or liquidize with a little of the liquid. Return the purée to the pan and stir into the liquid.

4 Stir in the cream and heat through gently, without letting the soup come to the boil. Check the seasoning, swirl in the butter, and serve at once.

La Saint-Martin

THE FEAST OF ST MARTIN

Hundreds of French villages and thousands of churches are named after St Martin, the dashing Roman soldier who, legend has it, once gave half his cloak to a shivering beggar. His feast on November 11th is now somewhat obscured by the fact that this is also a public holiday commemorating the end of World War I.

In the north and north-east of the country in particular, banquets honouring the saint invariably feature a goose as a *pièce de résistance*. They are also a perfectly timed opportunity to taste the season's new wines. This Martinmas goose pot-roast comes from the Lorraine.

Oie en Daube de la Saint-Martin

(GOOSE POT-ROAST)

serves 6

1 small goose, jointed
100g/3½oz rindless smoked streaky bacon, chopped
30g/1oz/¼cup flour
500ml/16fl oz/2cups dry white wine
2 bay leaves
a few sprigs each of parsley and thyme
1 large ripe tomato, blanched, peeled, deseeded and chopped
40g/1½oz butter
18 button onions, peeled and blanched
5ml/1teaspoon sugar
2 shallots, finely chopped
1 garlic clove, finely chopped
3tablespoons finely chopped flat-leaf parsley
salt and freshly ground black pepper

1 Heat a large heavy-based saucepan or casserole dish and sauté the bacon until crisp. Add the jointed goose and sauté until browned, turning the pieces over a few times. Pour off the fat.

2 Sprinkle with the flour, stir for a minute, then pour in the wine and top with enough water to just cover the pieces of goose. Add the bay leaves, herbs and chopped tomato. Season lightly with salt and pepper. Cover tightly and simmer gently over a low heat for a good two hours. Stir once after the first hour.

3 In a frying-pan, melt the butter over a moderate heat. Once it is hot, add the onions to the pan, sprinkle them with sugar and sauté them until they turn an even golden brown.

4 Stir the onions into the pot-roast and continue cooking, uncovered, for 10–15 minutes.

5 Combine the finely chopped shallots, garlic and parsley in a small bowl.

6 Remove the bay leaves and sprigs of herbs from the pot-roast and check the seasoning. Sprinkle with the shallot mixture and serve at once.

Saint Nicolas

ST NICHOLAS

On the night of December 5th, the eve of the feast of Saint Nicholas, young children in north and north-east France are unusually well-behaved. Before going to bed they put out their shoes and some straw in front of the chimney, for their patron saint and for the donkey he always rides on his travels. In return for this kind attention, Saint Nicholas traditionally leaves behind spiced biscuits shaped in his own image.

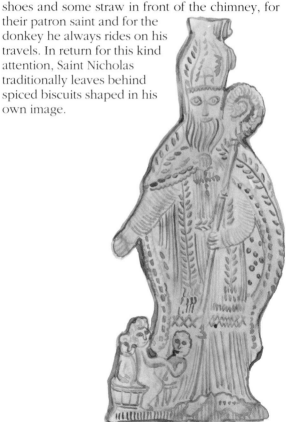

Pain d'Epice

SPICED BISCUITS

makes 14–20, depending on size

125g/4½oz/⅓cup runny honey
125g/4½oz/⅓cup molasses
75g/2½oz/⅓cup caster sugar
5ml/1teaspoon vanilla essence
125g/4½oz/½cup butter
1 large egg
400g/14oz/3½cups wholemeal flour
10ml/2teaspoons baking powder
pinch of salt
100g/3½oz/½cup ground almonds
finely grated zest of 1 lemon and 1 orange
10ml/2teaspoons ground cinnamon
5ml/1teaspoon ground nutmeg
5ml/1teaspoon aniseed

Glaze
75ml/5tablespoons/
   ⅓cup orange juice
7–8 tablespoons
   icing sugar

1 Combine the honey, molasses, caster sugar and vanilla essence in a saucepan. Heat gently until dissolved, then stir in the butter until melted. Leave to cool.
2 Work in the egg, flour and then the remaining ingredients. Mix into a dough, then cover and leave to rest overnight in a cool place.
3 Roll out the dough to about 1cm/½in thick. Using biscuit cutters, cut the dough into gingerbread men or heart shapes. Arrange the dough shapes on greased baking sheets and bake for 10–15 minutes in a preheated 200°C/400°F/gas6 oven until golden and just firm to the touch.
4 Remove from the oven. Make a glaze by combining the orange juice and icing sugar. Brush over the biscuits while they are still warm. Transfer to a rack with a palette knife and leave to cool.

Noël

CHRISTMAS

Christmas in France has always been both a religious and a family feast. In the old days the most significant, religious part of the celebrations took place on Christmas Eve, when the whole family would gather together for supper and to go to Midnight Mass. This was a happy reunion and friends and family would gather round the hearth and sing and tell stories. In keeping with the religious significance of the evening, the dishes shared were fairly simple – soups, breads, cakes, vegetables. Fish and snails were allowed but no meat was served. *Aligot*, eaten on Christmas Eve in the Auvergne, is made with the potatoes and cheese that are local everyday fare.

After the relative abstinence of Christmas Eve, large and elaborate meat courses were joyfully consumed the following day. People feasted on the region's most sumptuous dishes. The stuffed chicken recipe on the following pages comes from Gascony.

Aligot
(POTATO AND CHEESE PUREE)

serves 4–6
900g/2lb waxy potatoes
75g/2½oz/⅓cup butter
75ml/5tablespoons/⅓cup milk
100ml/4fl oz/½cup *crème fraiche* or thick cream
350g/12oz *tomme d'aligot* or young farmhouse
  Lancashire or Caerphilly, finely slivered
2 garlic cloves, finely chopped
20ml/1tablespoon/1½tablespoons good bacon fat
  (optional)
salt and freshly ground black pepper

1 Bring plenty of lightly salted water to the boil in a
large heavy-based saucepan. Add the potatoes,
reduce the heat and simmer gently until the
potatoes are soft but not disintegrating. Drain
carefully, then peel the potatoes as soon as they
are cool enough to handle.
2 Melt the butter in the pan over a low heat. Pass
the potatoes through a mouli, or mash them lightly
but thoroughly. Stir them into the melted butter,
then add the milk and cream and stir until
combined.
3 Work the slivered cheese into the purée a little
at a time, using a wooden spoon. Mix in the garlic,
and the bacon fat if using. Season generously with
pepper.
4 Continue stirring over a low heat for a good 5
minutes, until the cheese starts to make strings.
Serve at once.

La Poule au Pot Farcie

STUFFED CHICKEN

serves 12

1 very large corn-fed chicken, weighing
  approximately 2.3kg/5lb
4 large waxy potatoes, peeled and quartered
4 large leeks, trimmed, washed, and cut into thick
  segments

For the boiled beef

1 large marrow bone
550g/1¼lb lean braising steak, trimmed of visible
  fat, cut into 5cm/2in pieces
550g/1¼lb shin of beef, cut into 5cm/2in pieces
3 garlic cloves, peeled and halved
3 bay leaves
several sprigs of thyme
4 large carrots, peeled and cut into segments
4 medium turnips, trimmed, peeled and quartered
1 Spanish onion, studded with cloves
12 button onions, peeled
3 celery stalks, washed, trimmed and cut into
  segments
salt and freshly ground black pepper

For the chicken stuffing

150g/5½oz rindless dry-cured smoked ham
100g/3½oz day-old breadcrumbs, soaked in a little
  milk and squeezed
giblets from the chicken
75g/2½oz veal escalope
1 garlic clove
3 shallots
3tablespoons finely chopped parsley
2 medium eggs
salt and freshly ground black pepper

To serve
Tomato sauce (page 44–5)
mustard
strongly flavoured mayonnaise

gherkins
coarse sea salt

1 First prepare the boiled beef. In a stockpot large enough to take the meat *and* chicken, cover the marrow bone and meat with plenty of water, then add the garlic, bay leaves and thyme. Bring to the boil very slowly, skimming any grey scum that comes up.

2 Add the prepared vegetables and bring back to a gentle boil. Skim and season lightly with salt and pepper.

3 Meanwhile, prepare the stuffing for the chicken. Finely mince together or process all the ingredients. Stir in the eggs and season. Spoon the stuffing into the cavity and sew it up with a trussing needle and fine string, then truss the chicken with the string.

4 Place the chicken on top of the beef and vegetables. Cover and cook slowly for 2–2½ hours, skimming occasionally. Add the potatoes and leeks after one hour.

5 To serve, lift out the chicken and the beef with a slotted spoon. Arrange the beef on a large dish, reserving the marrow bone. Remove the strings from the chicken and place on top of the beef. Surround with the vegetables, discarding the onion studded with cloves, bay leaves and sprigs of thyme. Spoon out the marrow and dot it over the vegetables (or give it on a piece of toast to your most senior guest).

6 Check the seasoning of the stock. Strain through a fine sieve into a jug, reserving a little to moisten the meats and vegetables. Serve at once, with the jug of stock and the accompaniments.

Les Treize Desserts
(THIRTEEN CHRISTMAS SWEETS)

On Christmas Eve in Provence, families traditionally sat round a table laid with three white cloths, lit with three candles, for a ritual supper, *le gros souper*.

The meal was washed down with *vin cuit*, mulled wine, and ended with a magnificent spread of sweets and desserts – thirteen in all to represent Christ and his disciples – including dried and fresh fruits, almonds and walnuts, roast chestnuts, raisins, dates and prunes filled with marzipan, jams, quince paste (see recipe). Though the foods varied from village to village, always included were honeyed nougats, black or white, flavoured with pistachio or studded with pinenuts, and a sweet flavoured bread called *Pompe*.

Pompe
(PROVENÇAL CHRISTMAS BREAD)

serves6

250g/8½oz bread dough
40ml/2tablespoons/3tablespoons olive oil, plus
  extra for greasing
grated zest of 1 lemon and 1 orange
10ml/2teaspoons ground aniseed
85g/3oz/⅓cup caster sugar
2 medium eggs

1 Work into the bread dough the remaining ingredients, reserving a little egg yolk for glazing, mixed with 1tablespoon water in a small cup.
2 Roll out the dough into a circle about 2cm/¾in thick. Slit with a knife at regular intervals. Leave to rest in a warm place for a few hours.
3 Brush the dough lightly with egg glaze. Place on a greased baking sheet and bake in a preheated

190°C/375°F/gas5 oven for about 20 minutes, until cooked and golden. Serve warm or cold, with hot mulled wine.

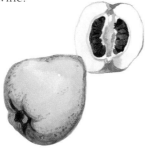

Pâte de Coings
(QUINCE PASTE)

makes 1.8kg/4lb
1kg/2¼lb unpeeled ripe quinces, quartered
125ml/4½fl oz/⅔cup water
5ml/1 teaspoon ground nutmeg
2 cloves
caster sugar

1 In a large saucepan, boil the quinces with the water, nutmeg and cloves until soft. Strain, discarding the cores and cloves. Purée, then weigh the pulp.
2 Pour the pulp into a clean saucepan. Add the same weight of caster sugar and cook gently for 30 minutes, stirring very frequently. The paste is cooked when it slides off a spoon in one piece. Pour into a tin and leave to get cold.
3 To serve, turn the paste out of the tin. Cut it into small circles, squares and lozenges and roll lightly in sugar. The paste keeps well if wrapped and chilled.

Le Réveillon de la Saint-Sylvestre et le Jour de l'An

NEW YEAR'S EVE AND NEW YEAR'S DAY

Whereas Christmas remains a genuine *fête de famille*, a decorous family celebration, New Year's Eve and New Year's Day have become an extravaganza of feasting. Of the rituals associated with the end of the old year and the start of the new, all that remain are decorative bunches of mistletoe. People spend their time at the table indulging in fine foods and wines. Oysters, foie gras, lobsters, champagne... no expense is spared.

Restaurants put up their prices and offer special menus – sometimes very special indeed. In the besieged, starving Paris of 1870, diners at the luxurious Chez Peter's had to make do with elephant escalopes and roasted bear supplied by the Zoo. A generation or so later, a more orthodox *Réveillon* menu featured a bisque of langoustine, turbot, pheasant soufflé, guinea fowl in curried sauce, a gratin of cardoons, orange fritters and a pineapple charlotte topped with pistachio zabaglione. *Bon appétit!*

Filets de Turbot au Champagne
(TURBOT WITH A CHAMPAGNE SAUCE)

serves 4

4 skinned turbot fillets, no less than 200g/7oz each
20ml/1tablespoon/1½tablespoons oil
100g/3½oz/½cup butter
3 shallots, finely chopped
115g/4oz button mushrooms, rinsed, patted dry
   and thinly sliced
20ml/1tablespoon/1½tablespoons chopped parsley
20ml/1tablespoon/1½tablespoons flour
100ml/4fl oz/½cup reduced fish stock boiled down
   from 200ml/7fl oz/¾cup
175ml/6fl oz/¾cup champagne or dry sparkling
   wine
150ml/¼pint/⅔cup thick cream
salt and white pepper

1 Heat the oil and a third of the butter in a heavy-based pan large enough to take the turbot fillets side by side. Over a low heat sauté the shallots for a few minutes, then stir in the prepared mushrooms and parsley and sauté until tender. Remove from the pan with a fish slice.

2 Season the flour with a small pinch of salt and a little pepper. Lightly dust the turbot fillets with the seasoned flour. Add half the remaining butter to the pan and carefully sauté the turbot fillets until lightly coloured on both sides.

3 Return the shallot mixture to the pan, with the reduced fish stock and half the champagne. Simmer very gently for a few minutes, then lift the fillets onto a heated serving dish. Keep warm.

4 Add the cream to the cooking liquid and stir over a low heat until hot. Stir in the remaining champagne, heat through and check the seasoning.

5 Swirl in the rest of the butter, stir, then pour over the turbot fillets. Serve at once.